MW00935962

THE
GHOSTLY TALES
OF
CHARLESTON

Published by Arcadia Children's Books
A Division of Arcadia Publishing
Charleston, SC
www.arcadiapublishing.com

Copyright © 2020 by Arcadia Children's Books
All rights reserved

Spooky America is a trademark of Arcadia Publishing, Inc.

First published 2020

Manufactured in the United States

ISBN 978-1-4671-9800-4

Library of Congress Control Number: 2020938906

Notice: The information in this book is true and complete to the best of our knowledge. It is offered without guarantee on the part of the author or Arcadia Publishing. The author and Arcadia Publishing disclaim all liability in connection with the use of this book.

All rights reserved. No part of this book may be reproduced or transmitted in any form whatsoever without prior written permission from the publisher except in the case of brief quotations embodied in critical articles and reviews.

Photo credits: used throughout Eugenia Petrovskaya/Shutterstock.com; used throughout Nataliia K/Shutterstock.com; used throughout In-Finity/Shutterstock.com; p. iv–1 the Hornbills Studio/Shutterstock.com; p. iv–1 Caso Alfonso/Shutterstock.com; p. iv–1 Ivakoleva/Shutterstock.com; p. iv–1 LDDesign/Shutterstock.com; p. iv–1 netsign33/Shutterstock.com; p. 4, 48, 84 basel101658/Shutterstock.com; p. 21 KsanaGraphica/Shutterstock.com; p. 63 Forgem/Shutterstock.com; p. 100 Jurgita Batuleviciene/Shutterstock.com; p. 10, 54, 88 Rassamee Design/Shutterstock.com; p. 16, 30, 58, 70, 94, 104 Wilqkuku/Shutterstock.com; p. 22, 64, 98 solarseven/Shutterstock.com; p. 38, 76 CloudOnePhoto/Shutterstock.com.

Spooky America

THE
GHOSTLY TALES
OF
CHARLESTON

ALLISON SINGER

...apted from *Haunted Charleston*, by Ed Macy and Geordie Buxton

ARCADIA
PUBLISHING

NORTH CAROLINA

SOUTH CAROLINA

GEORGIA

ATLANTIC OCEAN

9

12

10

CHARLESTON

14

6

11

5

7

15

2

16

4

1

3

8

13

TABLE OF CONTENTS & MAP KEY

Introduction

Hello, brave reader! Welcome to Charleston, South Carolina. In photographs of this historic city, you'll see splendid places: the College of Charleston, with its campus crawling in moss and ivy. The Citadel, a huge military fortress that stands tall and imposing. Centuries-old churches, majestic examples of the architecture of their time. What you won't see (or will you?): the ghosts.

And trust me, reader, there are *lots* of ghosts here in Charleston.

In this book, you'll read about real events that happened to real people. Few have heard these spine-tingling stories before. I've added no elements of mystery or intrigue to make the stories seem more frightening. I didn't have to. They're creepy enough simply as they are.

Many people throughout history have asked why the city of Charleston has so many ghosts. It's my opinion that a ghost is like a heavy fog: Once it settles, it isn't quick to leave. Charleston has entire neighborhoods that are filled with old houses, churches, and storefronts. Even the tiniest details, from the doorknobs to the lighting fixtures, remain exactly the same as they were hundreds of years ago. If you were a ghost, wouldn't you want to stick around the familiar things from when you lived? I know I would.

But hey, that's just my opinion. Perhaps after reading these tales, you'll uncover your own.

12 Glebe Street

Let's begin with the strange tale of the house at 12 Glebe Street. It was built in 1855, before the start of the Civil War. Over the years, what was once a stately home fell into a state of total disrepair. When the College of Charleston bought the house in 1966, school officials knew they had a lot of fixing-up to do before it would be ready for new residents to move in. But they didn't know just how extensive that fixing-up would have to be—or why. Some say they should have left the house alone.

Once the purchase of the house was complete, the school sent a crew to check out the home's condition. Inside, they found their first surprise: a maze. A previous tenant had gotten a bunch of plywood sheets and used them to cover all of the house's doors. The tenant had also covered all of the windows. Even the staircase was completely boarded up. WEIRD. The result? In an enormous, fifteen-room house, just one teensy bit of space was left to live in.

The college's crew was mystified and totally creeped out. Who would do this? And why? Were they hiding something? Or *from* something? Set on their plans to restore the home to good condition, the crew tore down all of the plywood, and renovations began.

Within a year or two, the house was all

fixed up and ready for new tenants. A young (unsuspecting) couple who worked at the college moved in. Scott and Rebecca Steinberg were thrilled to see their new home. It was so elegant and so close to work. They decided their bedroom would be the second-floor master suite, the one that faces out toward Glebe Street.

This was their first mistake. (Or, it could be argued, maybe their first mistake was moving into the house at all.) For it was in this room, in the late summer of 1968, that the Steinbergs realized why those plywood barriers had been installed so many years ago. To keep out a ghost.

It was in this room that they first saw him.

He made his appearance just after nine o'clock one night. Scott and Rebecca were in bed, reading. The reading lamps on both sides of the bed were on, so you can imagine that the room was pretty well lit.

And yet, in walked a ghost. He stood at the foot of their bed.

He was about six feet tall. The Steinbergs reported that he looked well dressed. He had on a suit with a collar, and a "fluffy" tie. He had short hair and seemed to be from "the Victorian period."

But his appearance wasn't the most striking thing about him. No, it wasn't the way he looked, the Steinbergs said. It was what he did—or, rather, *didn't* do.

The ghost looked at the Steinbergs. He tried to speak, but nothing came out. No words, not a sound. He could only move his lips, like an actor in a silent movie. After several seconds of trying, the ghost clearly got frustrated. He began to wildly swing his hands around, desperately trying to get his point across. The Steinbergs had NO idea what he was trying to say. After a few more moments, the ghost gave up. Disappointed, he dropped his hands down to his sides and left the room—through a solid plaster wall.

The Steinbergs were stunned.

The old house at 12 Glebe Street is now a guesthouse. (I bet the Steinbergs didn't stick around too long.) There aren't any people in the house year round to see the ghost and his attempts at telling his story (or asking his questions). Does the ghost still lurk in the walls and front bedroom? Does he still stand at the foot of the bed and try to speak? This mystery, along with who the ghost is and what his silent message may be, remains unsolved.

The Old Bicycle Shop

Most people know when they've seen a ghost. But what about weird feelings or experiences that you can't explain? Are those ghosts, too?

There are lots of ways for a ghost to appear in this world. People may see or hear a ghost. Sometimes people report *smelling* a ghost. (What could a ghost *possibly* smell like? I don't think I want to know.) In certain cases, people may "feel" a ghostly presence. Events like a quick drop in temperature can suggest that a ghost is near. But sometimes, for reasons unknown, a ghost cannot directly reveal that it's lurking nearby. It must remain in the shadows. So the ghost leaves clues, hoping someone will find them and care enough to figure out their meaning. Which is exactly what happened in what was once Brauer's Bicycle Shop, at 185 Calhoun Street.

The bicycle shop opened in 1965. It closed suddenly in 1971 when its owner, poor Mrs. Brauer, found herself in the wrong place at the wrong time during a botched robbery attempt. (Sadly, she met her end that night.) It then became part of the College of Charleston, who turned it into the college bookstore, which is where the students of the college get all the books they need for their classes.

Almost immediately, strange things began to happen, sometimes right in front of confused employees. So many unexplainable things have been reported at the shop that we could go on for pages. So we'll focus on the following event that happened many times between the years of 1972 and 1989.

Twice a year, before a new college semester began, new textbooks arrived by the truckload at the college bookstore. From American literature to zoology, each textbook was carefully shelved in its proper section. That was the only way to keep things organized! Soon, a stampede of students would descend on the little brick bookstore, eager to buy up all the books they needed for their classes.

Once the shelves were finally stocked, every last book in its place, the staff would leave the store, happy to enjoy the last few hours of their summer or winter break. But when they returned in the morning—one hour before the store was scheduled to open—they would find PANDEMONIUM. Their careful work had been completely undone! Instead of neatly organized shelves, the books were now stacked in teetering five-foot-tall towers all around the store. They were in no order whatsoever, and they were no longer on the shelves. They had been mixed up, shuffled about, and stacked, one atop the other, completely at random.

With precious few minutes before the doors opened and the students came pouring in, the panicked staff zipped and zoomed around the store, racing to get books back on shelves.

Was this the handiwork of the ghost of Mrs. Brauer, haunting what was once her beloved bicycle shop? That's the theory. If it *is* her ghost, she can't be seen, smelled, heard, or felt.

There's no drop in temperature, no strange noises, no feelings of "something" watching the employees.

But some believe that the stacks of books are her way of announcing that she remains hidden in the building. No one's sure why Mrs. Brauer feels the need to mess with her building's current tenants. Maybe it's just her way of saying, "Hey! I'm still here!"

1837 Bed and Breakfast

On we go to the 1837 Bed and Breakfast, at 126 Wentworth Street. It's a sweet little inn nestled in Harleston Village. That's just one block west of the College of Charleston. This cozy inn is a favorite among visitors to Charleston, offering a beautiful place to stay and delicious food to eat while exploring the city.

But hotel guests are not the only occupants here. You can probably guess what I'm getting at. Yes, 126 Wentworth Street is also home to a ghost.

His name? George. His age? Just nine years old.

George is not a frightening specter. In fact, he's known as one of Charleston's most playful ghosts. Guests report finding the indent of his small feet on the end of their bed when they wake or hearing him playing just outside. In 2003, two guests from Michigan said their dresser and bathroom doors opened and closed throughout the night. Could this have been some of George's mischief?

In 1999, a woman from California noted an empty rocking chair outside her room—*rocking*. Then she heard the manager yell, "Stop!" And guess what? The chair immediately came to a halt. Later, the woman asked the manager about it, and the manager said, casually, "Oh, it's just George playing again."

Despite his playful nature, George's story is filled with sadness. When he was alive, he and his parents were slaves. Back in the early 1830s, when slavery was still legal in Charleston, George and his parents moved into the house at 126 Wentworth Street. George's family was owned by the man who built the house. They were sent to work at the house for the family who lived there, the Holders. George's job was to feed Mr. Holder's two horses and wash them down each day. Occasionally, George would go into town to run errands.

After a time, George's mother and father were sold to a planter from Virginia, and they left 126 Wentworth Street. George was left behind. He was devastated. He had nightmares. Once, he tried to escape to find his parents. He rode in the back of a wagon for hours. George eventually fell asleep— and when he woke up, he found himself right back in Charleston. He was returned to 126 Wentworth Street to work again in Mr. Holder's stable.

There are pretty much no records of George's life after the sale of his parents. Slaves were not allowed to read or write, making family records nearly impossible to find. No official records of George's death have ever been discovered. But many feel certain George's ghost now plays at the house where he once lived, his presence haunting—and delighting—the guests of the 1837 Bed and Breakfast.

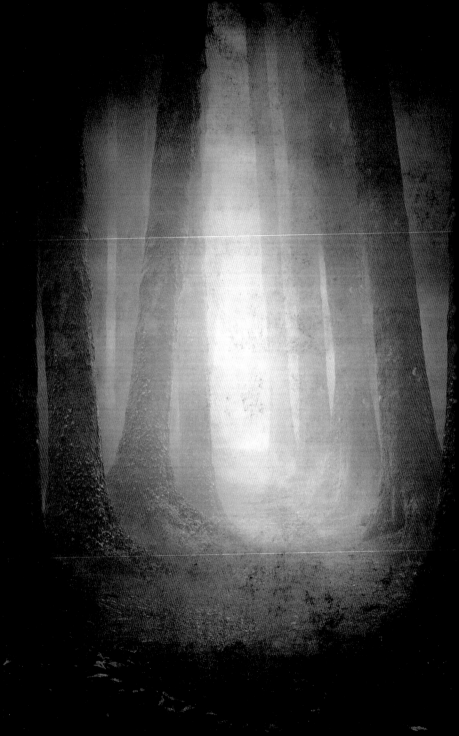

18 Montagu Street

Near the 1837 Bed and Breakfast in Harleston Village (one of Charleston's oldest neighborhoods) stands the house at 18 Montagu Street. It's a large, stately home that was built by an important local businessman. Back then the home was a landmark said to have housed George Washington during a a famous visit to Charleston in the spring of 1791.

Like many large eighteenth-century houses, 18 Montagu Street is no longer a single-family residence. Instead, it has been sliced and diced into apartments, often used by students at the College of Charleston. These students and their fellow residents are the ones who tell the spooky and haunty tales of the ghost that lurks in this elegant and historic home.

Charleston is a coastal city, and coastal cities often bear the brunt of hurricanes, tropical storms, and terrible flooding. Charleston's being doing it for hundreds of years.

The deadly hurricane of 1813 especially had a huge impact on the South Carolina coast. It wasn't the strongest storm to hit the city, but with hurricanes, that's not all that matters. The placement of the storm's eye matters, as does how high (or low) the tides are. Those forces are what can really decide how devastating a storm will be.

Nearly twenty people died in the storm of 1813. And the city's shipping industry—a major part of this port city's strength—was battered and useless for months afterward.

It was a sticky night in August as the winds gathered in strength. Their whooshing sounds soon turned to howling cries accompanied by whipping branches and crashing trees. From inside 18 Montagu Street, the Walters family and their servants huddled in fear. The house was creaking wildly. It sounded like a ship being torn apart.

Mr. Walters saw that the glass windows offered very little protection from the violence of the storm. He ordered everyone to run to the house's lowest level, where there was a nearly empty brick room with a large fireplace. The room was used as the servants' quarters.

Mr. Walters's three young daughters were terrified of the storm. They gathered around their nanny, Mary—known to them as "Miss Mary." At the insistence of Mr. Walters, the girls clung to Miss Mary in the center of the room, right in front of the brick fireplace. It seemed to him the safest spot. Sadly, he was wrong.

Mary did her best to calm the girls and soothe their fears. She had never heard the rain so strong and the wind so angry before. She hid her own terror while she comforted the little girls she loved so much.

Suddenly, the chimney of the fireplace began to crumble. Bricks began to fall. Mary pulled the children closer to her and fell on top of them, protecting them from the chaos. The children were saved, but poor Mary was not. She was sixty-six years old.

Many years passed. The hurricane of 1813

was largely forgotten, just another storm in Charleston's history of dangerous weather.

In 1988, College of Charleston student Shari Oswald lived on the top floor of 18 Montagu Street, in a one-room apartment.

On a Friday evening in December, Shari was getting ready to go out with some friends. She was seated in front of a long mirror, brushing her hair, looking forward to a fun night. That's when Shari saw her.

Suddenly, standing behind her, the form of a woman took shape. The woman had a very serious look on her face. She wore a loose, white dress and a white bandana on her head. Her hands were folded across her chest.

While looking at Shari in the mirror's reflection, the woman gave a very small nod. She then closed her eyes and turned away. Before Shari even had the chance to turn around, the woman disappeared into the wall of the apartment. Shari was freaked out. But also very curious as to who that woman was.

The upstairs apartment where Shari lived is where most ghostly sightings have occurred at 18 Montagu Street, although other apartments have had their share.

According to the current owner of the property, Shari's apartment was once a small ballroom used during fancy parties back in the old days. As a servant in the house, Mary would have tended to the family's guests, helping pour cocktails in that ballroom, and delivering fancy snacks (called canapés, for you fancy readers).

Her three young charges would definitely have wanted to play in that room, whether or not there was a party. We can imagine Mary looking on, smiling, as the three small Walters daughters danced around the room and pretended to be some of the wonderful guests, like President George Washington.

And despite the passing of time and the many changes that have come to the house, Mary's ghost remains. She stays to make sure that everything is all right at 18 Montagu Street.

CHAPTER
5

The Charleston Orphan House

In October 1918, the orphans and nurses at the Charleston Orphan House, built in 1790, faced their greatest challenge. An epidemic of influenza—the flu—had infected more than two hundred orphans. Many of the children were very sick. Some died.

Miss Lesesne was the person in charge. She called in every staff member she could to help care for the children.

With the staff occupied, the few orphans who weren't sick played outside by themselves, unsupervised. Their favorite game? Taking cardboard boxes out of the trash and using them to make tents. The children would pretend to be on camping trips. From inside their tents, they'd pretend to fish or roast food over an imaginary fire. They'd collect sticks and twigs to use as their fishing rods.

Their game may seem harmless to you, reader, but the staff HATED it. Why? Visitors would travel from far away to see the orphanage, which was in a beautiful old building. When they arrived, however, they'd see cardboard boxes and sticks all over the ground. It looked like a trash heap, not a beautiful building. Whenever children were caught digging through the trash, it was assumed they were in search of old cardboard to make a tent. Those who were caught were punished. But the children continued their game, as children do.

One evening, a group of kids made their tent. At some point, it caught fire. Some say the children set it aflame on purpose, as a sort of prank. But we'll never really know.

It's said that the orphans watched the burning tent from a hiding spot nearby, waiting for someone to come and put out the fire. But no one came. Busy caring for more than two hundred sick children, none of the staff members noticed the flames.

The fire grew. It leapt from cardboard tent to cardboard tent. The flames could be seen from far away. Black smoke billowed up and into the orphanage itself through windows and vents.

According to orphan house records, four children died. It was a miracle the number was so low but a tragedy nonetheless. It's those children whose spirits may now be haunting the site's current residents: the College of Charleston students at Joe E. Berry Hall.

Fast-forward about seventy years.

In the first few years after its construction in 1988, Berry Hall had a strange plague. It wasn't a plague of bugs, or germs, or anything like that. It was a plague of false fire alarms. Every time a fire alarm rang—which was almost always in the late hours of a quiet night, of course—the city fire marshal and his crew would respond rapidly. They always assumed it was an emergency. How could they not? They had to hurry over and search every room for signs of smoke. Meanwhile, students rushed outside, often in their pajamas. Some were scared. But many of them were just really annoyed.

The police and fire department wanted to know who was causing all the false alarms. Berry Hall residents were questioned again and again to see who was pulling the fire alarms. WHO DID IT?

The fire marshal even tried a sneaky trick to catch the culprits. He had his team sprinkle an invisible dust on the fire-alarm handles. When someone pulled the handle, the dust would stick to their hands. A firefighter could shine a special light on the suspected students' hands and voila! The dust would reveal the culprit. But no one was ever caught dusty-handed.

Then, in the mid-1990s, another strange occurrence. Students reported being kept awake by a haunting sound: the distant squeals and laughter of small children. Maybe the sound of happy kids doesn't seem all that scary to you, but the eerie sounds were heard traveling through the halls, stairwells, and air-conditioning vents of Berry Hall in the middle of the night.

The students weren't the only ones to hear the noises. Visitors staying in the dorms during summer break reported hearing them, too. The college offers new students and their parents a night's stay in Berry Hall before they go on a tour of the historic campus. But after a night hearing children laughing in the distance, many guests don't show up for the tours. Some of the parents have even called their tour guides with furious complaints: "Where are the parents of these children running wild in the middle of the night?" The tour guides don't know what to say.

In the summer of 2003, the college began a renovation of Berry Hall. The air-conditioning system—which was often blamed for the high-pitched, voice-like sounds that people heard in the night—was replaced with more efficient, modern technology. The fire-alarm system was modified as well.

When Berry Hall reopened, do you think the strange occurrences stopped? Nope. In fact, the number of false fire alarms increased.

There's a concrete parking lot where the great entrance to the Charleston Orphan House once stood. Stand there for a little while, and you may hear the voices of children laughing. Stand there a bit longer, and there's a chance you'll catch them singing "Ring Around the Rosie" in the distance. Their lives ended in tragedy, for sure. But witnesses say the children don't sound sad at all. To some, it sounds like the ghosts are celebrating.

CHAPTER 6

The South Carolina Military Academy

In 1822, the South Carolina government decided to build a fortress in Charleston. It would serve as a warning to anyone who even thought about harming the city. The fortress would send a loud message to the world, one of strength and determination. So it was named after the Greek word for "fortress." It was called the Citadel.

In 1842, the South Carolina Military Academy opened at the Citadel. The school soon became known for its incredibly high standards and strict military discipline. (Think: lots of yelling and scrubbing floors with toothbrushes if you got in trouble.) The towering fortress and the intimidating school were a match made in heaven—or maybe somewhere else entirely . . . As its reputation grew with each passing year, so did the school's attendance.

Sixty years later, in the early 1900s, the academy had taken on more students than the Citadel could hold. It moved from the original fortress to a new, bigger location. (Though, as you'll soon find out, many of the college's mysterious secrets—and spirits—stuck with the school even after it moved. But we'll save that for a later chapter, shall we?)

It was at the military college's new campus that cadet Will Hunter suffered a terrible fate: He died in 1966. He had been a student in First Battalion. After his death, Will's spirit was believed to have cursed the room he had lived in: Room 1423. This was all but confirmed when Padgett Yarborough, a junior who lived in 1423 just four years after Will, also died, in a car accident.

Over time, the stories of Will Hunter, Padgett Yarborough, and the cursed room faded away. That is, until 1980, just before Thanksgiving. It was then that a dim green light appeared to Pat Finch and Bruce Sutton of room 1123—exactly three floors below 1423.

Their first experience with the dim glow freaked the roommates out.

It appeared hovering in the corner of the room, according to the cadet who saw it first. He could hardly believe his eyes. Confused, he woke his roommate. He had to know if his roommate could see the light as well, or if it was only in his imagination. The second boy confirmed the sight. Despite being scared, the cadets were also really curious. What *was* this? What should they do? But they wondered for too long. Before they could come to any decision, it faded away.

After the Christmas break, the green light returned. This time, it showed up in the wee hours of the morning—at about 3:00 a.m. The light was pretty small. I mean, totally creepy, sure. But not terrifying. Not scary enough to send the students running out of their room.

As the light began appearing more and frequently, the roommates started inviting their friends to come over and see it.

Students piled into the room to see the tiny green glow. One cadet turned on the overhead light to see if the glow would disappear. The green light became dimmer but it stuck around. The cadet turned the light off, and the green glow got brighter. One cadet thought to ask it a question. "Who are you?" he asked. Unsurprisingly, the green light did not respond.

The cadets asked lots more questions but got no response until someone thought to give the light some options. He asked, "Are you a spirit? Nod up and down if you are a spirit, and side to side if you are not."

To the boys' shock and amazement (and, frankly, to some of their horror), the green light moved up and down! *They could communicate with it!* They would have to ask the light yes-or-no questions in order to receive responses. Some of the more nervous cadets stayed as far away from the green light as they could. Others got right up close. And still others turned and fled out the door.

The braver cadets stayed in the room and began round after round of interrogations. Several boys stood on chairs and waved their hands through the green light to try to find out where it was coming from. They never found an explanation.

The students continued their questioning. They learned that the green light was a cadet who had never graduated. It couldn't tell the boys its name, though. Or a reason *why* it never graduated. As the boys interrogated the light, it seemed to grow bored and tired. Then it simply disappeared.

The green light began to appear more regularly. One week in February 1981 saw the light return each and every night. Dozens of people came to see it including the college's public relations officer, Lieutenant Colonel Daniel Cooke.

Lots of students were interviewed about what they saw. One 1982 Citadel graduate said:

> *The light would disappear from time to time and then, after several seconds the light would flash again . . . when it appeared the third time it seemed to be floating in mid-air, this time in the form of a concentrated sphere.*

Many witnesses who communicated with the light believed it to be a floating class ring, but when asked if that was the case, the green light moved from side to side as if shaking its head.

This phenomenon was creepy, there's no doubt about that. But it was also . . . so *odd*. Some suggested that the green light was an elaborate hoax on the school and the students, and that it was made by laser holography or fiber optics. But remember, readers, this was 1981. These were the days before laser pens and cell phones. There weren't tons of sophisticated electronics lying around. A consistent dim green light with no obvious source would have been hard to pull off. Cadets looked around the walls, ceiling, and floor of the room for something—anything— that could explain the light but found nothing.

The green light made news in the *National Enquirer* newspaper that year. That was the very peak of its popularity. But its continued appearances in room 1123 eventually stopped without warning.

To this day, nobody has ever been able to prove or disprove the existence of the green light phantom. Was it a hoax? Or a message from a long-gone cadet? Was it Will Hunter or Padgett Yarborough? We'll likely never know for sure. What do you think?

The Embassy
Suites Hotel

After the South Carolina Military Academy left the original Citadel building, the fortress remained abandoned for seventy-five years. (That is, with the exception of a few government offices and a military museum on the ground floor.) Eerie and crumbling, it would likely have been torn down if the Hilton Hotels Corporation hadn't stepped in with a plan. In the mid-1990s, the old Citadel was reopened as an Embassy Suites Hotel.

But the military college's haunted history stayed with the building, even after the students and faculty were long gone. Which is weird, perhaps, but still true. Because there, on the second floor, lingers the spirit of a young cadet.

According to many eyewitness accounts from guests and hotel staff alike, the young cadet wears the military college's uniform—a gray jacket—and stands about five-and-a-half feet tall. It's hard to focus on any part of his appearance, however, other than one particularly strange and unnerving physical feature. It has caused employees to quit on the spot. It has caused guests to check out in the middle of the night.

Are you sure you want to know what it is?

OK, you've been warned.

The top of his head is missing.

According to the accounts of stunned housekeepers and horrified guests, it looks as if the spirit's head has been shaved off right above his eyebrows. Surprisingly, no one describes the sight as truly gross. But everyone agrees that it is definitely freaky.

Dr. Anna Fletcher, a heart surgeon from Brussels, Belgium, reported seeing the nearly headless ghost in September 2003. She awoke suddenly around 3:00 a.m. and "felt like someone was standing over me, watching me sleep," she said.

She looked around the dark room, waiting for her eyes to adjust. And then she saw him. Not too far away from her bed stood a young man in a gray jacket. She was scared, for sure, but she was also concerned for the poor guy. "He looked frightened," she said.

Dr. Fletcher shot out of bed. The young man stood directly between her and the door. If she was going to get out of the room, she was going to crash right into him. Instead, she ran right *through* him.

In a phone interview, Dr. Fletcher said:

> *Since it happened, I cannot get his face out of my mind. He was so frightened and confused, like he had just dropped out of the sky. Once I saw the shape of his head, I knew that he was . . . not alive. Seeing the image of a young man missing such an integral body part . . . I had to run. I could not comprehend it. I still cannot comprehend it.*

After escaping her room, Dr. Fletcher ran down the hotel stairs and straight to the front desk—in her pajamas. She recounted her story to the night clerk, who gave her a robe and called a cab to take her to the Francis Marion

Hotel next door. There, she spent the last few hours of the night wide awake, waiting for the dawn to arrive.

What she didn't know? The Francis Marion Hotel has a ghost of its own.

The Francis
Marion Hotel

In the early 1930s, a young man named Ned Cohen was visiting Charleston from New York City. It was a buisness trip, and his company had arranged for him to stay at the relatively new Francis Marion Hotel. His room was on the tenth floor.

Ned's trip was for work, sure, but he may have been looking for a long lost love. People say his heart was broken beyond repair.

As Ned looked out over the city lights that night, he would have felt the warm Charleston breeze through his open window. Perhaps he stumbled. Perhaps he leapt. The truth, as with so many of these stories, can never be known for sure. But what we do know is this: the large window in his room was wide open, the silk drapes blowing in the wind, when the body of poor Ned was found on the street below.

Ned's body now lies in a cemetery near Cooperstown, New York, eternally at rest. But his soul? Not resting at all. It wanders part of the Francis Marion Hotel to this day.

Occasionally, a cold wind whips open the window of Ned's old hotel room on the tenth floor. Guests report windowpanes that rattle, and silk drapes that billow into the room shaped like, is it arms? Reaching for the terrified guests? Indeed.

Ned Cohen's spirit also appears to some in the halls of the Francis Marion. He is reported to have a blank stare on his face, and he seems like he's about to ask a question. Apparently, he has no way to voice it, for his question remains unasked to this day.

The Marlboro Apartments

One April night in 1987, Geoffrey Keith got home to his apartment at 140 Queen Street and couldn't find the light switch. It wasn't where he remembered it to be. Which...made no sense at all. As he felt his way along the smooth wall and walked farther into the home he thought he knew, he noticed another strange thing. Not only had the light switch moved—the furniture had been rearranged as well.

He stumbled through the dark toward the bathroom, where he knew there was a night-light. But instead he found a white wax candle. Worried that someone had broken into his apartment—and was maybe still there—Geoffrey called out. But there was no response. He backed out of the bathroom and toward the open front door. Just before exiting, he turned his head . . .

As a medical student, very little could scare Geoffrey. Blood and guts? No big deal. Sickness and death? Been there, done that. But that night in April 1987, Geoffrey saw something in his apartment that sent him running down Queen Street, into his car, and far away.

The history of the building that was the Marlboro Apartments goes back to at least 1852. Originally, the building housed Roper

Hospital, one of the first surgical hospitals in Charleston. It opened in response to a yellow fever epidemic. Throughout a hundred years, Roper Hospital survived terrible disease outbreaks and natural (and man-made) tragedies including an earthquake, a tornado, several hurricanes, and three major wars.

The original building was nearly torn down after the great earthquake of 1886, which killed two patients and injured 125 others. But it wasn't until 1952 that the hospital was sold and converted into apartments—the Marlboro Apartments.

When Geoffrey walked out of his bathroom in the dark that evening, he reported hearing a low moan. As he slowly turned, he saw more burning candles lighting up a brutal scene: a doctor was performing surgery *in Geoffrey's apartment*. The patient, dressed in a military uniform, lay on an old table. A nurse wiped down the patient's wet, dirty forehead as the ghostly surgeon amputated his leg. Geoffrey dared not make eye contact with any of them as he ran out the door.

Word of Geoffrey's chilling experience spread like wildfire among medical and scientific communities. Some groups, including members of a laboratory at Duke University in Raleigh, North Carolina, made plans to investigate. It was suspected that what Geoffrey had seen may have been some sort of portal into the old hospital. But unfortunately, further investigation would never happen.

The Marlboro Apartments were destroyed by Hurricane Hugo two years later, taking any shreds of evidence along with them.

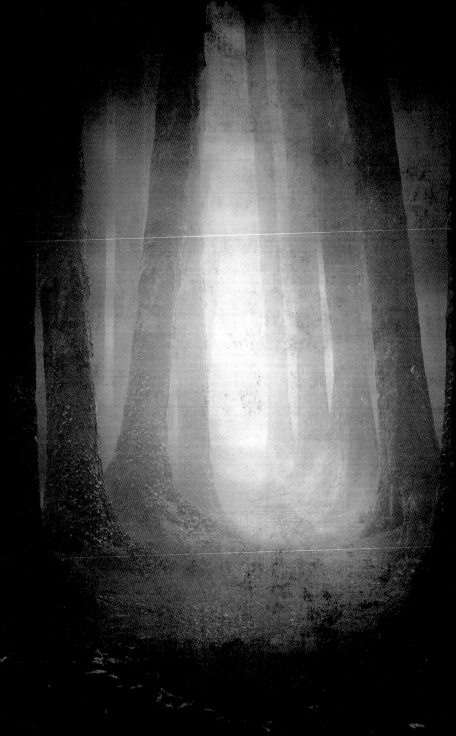

Pawleys Island

Shall we take a break from blood-and-guts and hear a story with a more uplifting ending? I've got just the one.

The tale of the Gray Man is a weird one for sure. Though he can be an unsettling sight, those who encounter him are likely to find themselves grateful in the end.

The Gray Man was last seen in September 1989. James and Elena Cordray were walking on the beach near their home on Pawleys Island. Pawleys Island is on the coast of South Carolina, about sixty miles northeast of Charleston. The sun was starting to set when they saw something in the water. It was a man, walking in the shallow ocean surf. At least, he appeared to be a man, they thought. A gray man. He had the general shape of a human. But he had no facial features that they could make out.

Though they were startled to see him, the Cordrays knew exactly who he was and why he had chosen to show himself. As longtime residents of the island, they had heard about him for years. The Gray Man shows up only when a brutal storm is on its way. His message is simple and serious: "See me and leave—now!"

The Cordrays heeded his warning. They immediately got in their car and headed inland, leaving behind the home they loved so much and everything in it. They drove straight to

Kentucky, without stopping, to stay with relatives until danger had passed.

To most people, these actions may seem a little irrational, even a little nuts. But the folks who live along the South Carolina coast, especially on Pawleys Island, know better. To them, the Cordray's actions were perfectly logical and sane. There was no choice. They had to leave.

Hurricane Hugo hit the island just fifty hours later.

Scientists have been studying hurricanes in detail for only about 100 years. Before the invention of TVs and the Internet, people who lived along the coast got about four hours' notice of a hurricane—if they were lucky. Sailors at sea usually rushed in early to warn waterfront cities like Charleston.

In 1989, Hurricane Hugo killed seventy-six people, half of them in South Carolina. The storm's winds reached 160 miles per hour. A tidal surge of up to twenty feet carried boats far inland, and submerged and destroyed homes for miles.

When James and Elena Cordray returned home to Pawleys Island, four days after they had left, they expected to find their neighborhood in shambles—and boy did they ever. But what they *didn't* expect to see was their house, standing in perfect condition among the rubble and destruction.

Not one shingle had come off their roof. Every window remained perfectly intact. If the local Pawleys Island newspaper is to be believed, even a beach towel remained hanging from the deck, *facing the ocean.*

This is the legacy of the Gray Man. It has been passed from one South Carolinian to another for at least two hundred years. "If you are chosen to see me," it says, "then take the giant leap of faith and leave immediately." Many have seen the Gray Man and decided not to go. We can only guess how many of them lived to regret their choice. . . .

The Stone House

Say hello to the Stone House, at 118 Folly Road on James Island. Built in the 1920s of heavy gray stones, it looks like a traditional home you'd see in the English countryside. The house is stately and solid. But inexplicable things lurk inside.

The Stone House has gained a reputation over the years as a haunted house, and not one of those cheesy ones that leaves you a little disappointed and wanting your money back.

It's a den of paranormal activity that scares anyone who lives there. As a result, it is almost always for sale. It is said that potential buyers have been scared away by the house's legacy before even seeing it in person.

The ghostly occurrences that have taken place in the Stone House range from kind of creepy to downright terrifying. Former residents speak of an area in the hallway that is always cold, no matter the season or outside temperature. (Remember: cold spots, sometimes forty degrees colder than the surrounding area, are thought to be signs of a spirit hanging around.) Several owners have reported to a newspaper that they smell heavy perfume that they don't recognize.

Ghost sightings have also been reported by residents. Some have seen the shadow of a tall man. Others have seen a little girl. Another sighting was of a woman with a 1920s-style haircut. And residents and neighbors all report seeing ghosts hanging out with (living) guests during house parties.

One of the strangest occurrences was reported by *The Post & Courier* newspaper on October 28, 1991. The alleged incident took place the previous winter, and it was told to the newspaper by Roland Cardwell, one of the house's former owners. According to Cardwell, his daughter had bought a bicycle and stashed it away in the attic. She planned to give it to a loved one as a Christmas gift.

One evening, she was thinking about how to get such a cumbersome gift downstairs without anyone noticing. Then she went outside to grab some smaller presents from her car. Suddenly, she heard a loud noise in the house. She rushed back in and found the bike on the first floor, standing perfectly on its kickstand.

She nervously thanked the spirit who so kindly helped her get the bike down.

Then, she left.

In a recent interview, one Charlestonian reported seeing something odd at the Stone House while she passed by in a car.

At the time, nobody was living in the house. A "For Sale" sign stood on the lawn near the busy street. It was night. The woman was in the passenger seat of her friend's car. As they passed the Stone House, she saw a shadowy figure standing in one of the attic windows, staring down at the car. And there was light streaming from the windows. But not white light. No, this light was blood red.

The driver of the car turned around so they could pass the house again. But this time the house was completely dark and empty. The blood-red light was gone. There was no sign of any people—living or dead—inside.

What is causing these events? Who are these figures and spirits seen in and around the Stone House? Theories abound. Some think the house's builder and original owner, John Doran, is haunting the house as he watches over his property. Another theory involves a little girl who was in a car accident on Folly Road.

More theories will arise as long as the Stone House stands, and especially whenever that "For Sale" sign makes its next foreboding appearance on the front lawn.

The Second
Presbyterian Church

Edwin Rose was a good man. He was also a longtime member of the Second Presbyterian church. One night in November 1979, Edwin helped chaperone a sleepover at the church for a youth group. He was out among the gravestones at dusk, making sure none of the more mischievous kids were still outside in the cemetery. It was on his return to the church building that he was caught off guard by a strange figure. It was angelic, with a white light that seemed to be glowing from within the figure. It was striking and peaceful in the darkening Charleston night.

At first, Edwin thought he was looking at the ghost of a woman. The figure wore a long robe that went down to the tops of its feet, and on its head was a pile of long, curly hair.

Edwin was captivated. He froze in the middle of the churchyard path, unable to stop staring at the illuminated spirit. Slowly the light dissolved into the night.

Edwin knew he had seen a ghost. But whose ghost was it? Edwin, always a curious fellow, had to find out. He was a devoted member of the church and loved to learn about its history. He decided to look through the church archives for clues. Feverishly, he researched church figures from past two hundred years.

He found a photograph of an old oil painting. It showed a former church pastor, Reverend Thomas Smyth. He had been painted with long, curly hair and a long robe—down to the tops of his feet, just like the spirit's smock.

Reverend Smyth was a nineteenth-century Scottish pastor of the Second Presbyterian Church. He took his role as church pastor very seriously. It didn't matter if he was preaching a sermon, or casually visiting members of his congretation, he always dressed the same: in long robes and a curly powdered wig. It was the same uniform of a British barrister, or lawyer.

What most people hear about Reverend Smyth is that he had an enormous library of books. They were all collected from his travels to different parts of Europe. But what Frederick Adolphus Porcher, another Charlestonian, remembered about Reverend Smyth is a bit different. He remembered him to be quite a talker—he'd talk your ear off if you'd let him. According to Frederick, Reverend Smyth wasn't really all that smart, or all that well-read. Seems he just talked a lot to make it look like he was. "His talk was not always to the point," said Frederick. This would prove to be true especially toward the end of Reverend Smyth's life.

Back to Edwin Rose, who wanted to learn more about Reverend Smyth, and to find out why his ghost had stuck around the churchyard of Second Presbyterian. He continued searching the church's archives for clues.

Edwin flipped through countless pages and pamphlets and books in the archive. Finally, he found a volume in Reverend Smyth's handwriting. It included notes, letters, and Reverend Smyth's thoughts. When the reverend had died, it seemed, he had passed the book down to his granddaughter, Louisa. Edwin learned a lot from the book, including the following:

The Second Presbyterian Church was established near downtown Charleston by mainly English, Scottish, and Irish families. The building was completed in 1811 and dedicated on April 3 of that year. It was nestled among marshy tidal creeks behind the Cooper River. From the river you could catch a peek of it through the oak trees.

Reverend Thomas Smyth was the church's fifth pastor, and the longest-serving pastor in the church's history. He was pastor for forty-two years, including through the Civil War. In fact, during the Civil War, he donated the church's bells to be melted down and made into cannons. (The bells were not replaced until 2004.)

The Civil War may have taken its toll on the reverend. His later journal entries make clear that his health wasn't so great. For forty-two years, the pastor had helped lay to rest Presbyterian families in the graveyard next to the church. In 1873, he died and lay among them.

We know now that Reverend Smyth probably had Alzheimer's disease in his final years. Then, the people around him called it "old man's disease." No longer of sound mind, his sermons remained long, but the community listening to them wasn't quite sure what he was saying. Some think he was simply talking gibberish. Others suspect he was having a conversation with the ghosts of the dead who lay buried in his churchyard.

In his notes and letters, Reverend Smyth copied down a poem by the poet Robert Southey. Part of it reads:

My thoughts are with the Dead, with them
I live in long-past years,
Their virtues love, their faults condemn,
Partake their hopes and fears,
And from their lessons seek and find
Instruction with an humble mind.

But again back to Edwin Rose. What he saw that November night was the pastor who helped lead the Second Presbyterian Church for a generation. Because of his otherworldly glow, many members of the church believe he is a kind and angelic spirit, with no plan to harm or scare people. They believe he sacrificed going to heaven to stay on Earth, near his beloved Charleston church and the people he had once tended to—and their children, grandchildren, and generations to come.

Drayton Hall

Let's continue on our journey through the ghosts of Charleston by moving along to Drayton Hall.

Drayton Hall is an estate house in Charleston. In the 1980s, three people claim to have seen a man peering from the upstairs window or walking down the avenue of oaks planted there. Many believe that this is the ghost of William Henry Drayton himself.

William died mysteriously at age 37, in the same year that his mysterious father also died mysteriously. (Lots of mystery here.) The estate was passed to William's younger brother. Once all of the family members had died, did William's ghost return to reclaim the property that he felt was rightfully his? Some believe this to be true.

Let's learn more about William Henry Drayton. He was born in 1742. His father, John Drayton, was a builder. William was the first Drayton son, and he was educated across the Atlantic, in England. Though he went on to political fame as a congressman and was generally well liked by the public, he was a disappointment to at least one person: his father. Some say William thought that his father had left him out of his will, which would mean William was never going to inherit the family estate at all.

Only William and his closest friends know the true story of his death. He died in Philadelphia, and it's possible that Drayton had enemies there. He could have been defeated in a pistol duel, perhaps. Another theory is that his friends sent word home to William's family that he had passed away suddenly of an illness in order to spare William's reputation. Or the cause of death may have been much darker and much more secret than that. After all, it's rather suspicious that William's father died in the same year, right? Does one death have to do with the other? How are the two connected?

Whatever the cause of William's death may be, the three sightings of his ghost show this much to be true: his spirit may be wandering Drayton Hall and the land he can finally claim as his own.

The Resurrection Tree

The Resurrection Tree is an old crape-myrtle tree on the site of the First Scots Presbyterian Church. The exact age of the tree is not known. It was once a thick-trunked tree, providing shade and beauty during hot Charleston summers. It is a silent, stately tree that stood proud as the parishioners passed it on their way into church each week.

On a September morning in 1938, a tornado ripped across the Peninsula from the Ashley

River. It destroyed the sheds in the City Market and killed over forty people. It also claimed another victim: the beautiful crape-myrtle tree. It was pulled from the earth and dropped broken and battered on Meeting Street.

Weeks after the tornado had passed, some members of the First Scots Presbyeterian church planted the roots and severed trunk of the crape myrtle. They hoped that, over many years, it would grow again into the beautiful creature it once was. At the very least, they felt at peace having rescued the dead tree from the street and returned it to the earth.

Churchgoers were gobsmacked when the tree bloomed again the very next summer. A miracle! (Seriously. That really shouldn't have happened.)

The tree became the talk of the town. "How can that tree…bloom?" people wondered in amazement.

The tree had a fan base. Charlestonians loved it and admired it. Sixteen summers passed, and each year the blooms came back, right on schedule. Then, Mother Nature had her vengeance once again. Three hurricanes slammed Charleston in the 1950s. The third—Hurricane Gracie—tore the branches right off of the crape myrtle in September 1959. Only its trunk was left. Charlestonians were devastated.

But then . . . One day the following spring, a little boy walking with his mother saw something. He told his mama to look at the tree that had "blown down." The stump had transformed. The branches were growing back! AGAIN. Would the tree bloom again? Surely not. But by the summer of 1960, blooms perched on the ends of those new branches. (Again—this is really not normal.)

The tree did just fine for another twenty years or so. Then, in the winter of 1979, something happened that almost *never* happens in the Lowcountry. An ice storm hit the Carolina coast. This is a type of weather Charleston people—and Charleston trees—are *really* not prepared for. The old crape myrtle tree finally died. For real this time. Someone cut it down. They wanted to prevent the stump from rotting, so they just filled it with concrete.

Did it really die? Could the beautiful, strong old tree actually be dead? As one church member put it, "it took Jack Frost to finally kill 'er." Yes, the tree was gone. But it wasn't forgotten.

Then, the following spring, a man walked to church with his young twins. It was a beautiful day, and he remembered a day twenty years earlier when he showed his mama that branches were growing from the tree that had "blown down." Rushing into church, he heard his daughter say, "Look, Daddy!"

There he saw, for the second time in his life, new growth springing from something thought dead. Four new shoots were reaching up from around the concrete stump! Seeking the sunlight once again, this amazing tree had defied death—for the *third* time.

Dubbed "the Resurrection Tree," this giant defies explanation. Even the winds from Hurricane Hugo in 1989 were no match.

The crape myrtle still stands today as strong as ever. The tree may not be supernatural or paranormal, but who is to say it's not? What do you think?

Found Grounds, Part I

Sometimes, when ground is broken for a new building, more than dirt and rocks are unearthed. The Medical University of South Carolina (MUSC) discovered this in late 2001. From underneath a potter's field in Charleston, workers dug up thirty-three caskets. The caskets were 199 years old.

Records show that Charleston's largest public burial grounds were located on that spot until 1825. That's when the government took over the land to use for the military.

The area then became the Porter Military Academy in 1867. After that, it was used as a parade ground and athletic field. MUSC purchased the land in 1963. In 1968, as it began construction on its basic science building, the school discovered more than a *hundred* graves. MUSC asked the city to move the graves to a site on nearby James Island, but no details or official records remain. We don't know if those buried folks were ever moved.

Then, in 2001, MUSC wanted to build its Children's Research Institute. It hired a company to do research and field investigations. This is when the thirty-three caskets, containing thirty-three bodies, were found.

Markers and names were never found with the caskets. Who were these people? What happened to them? In March 2003, the remains of the bodies were buried nearby. A plaque near St. Luke's Chapel (which sits across from the new Children's Research Institute) marks the new gravesite.

One can only imagine how many spirits lurk in the area and how they must feel about being disturbed from their long slumber.

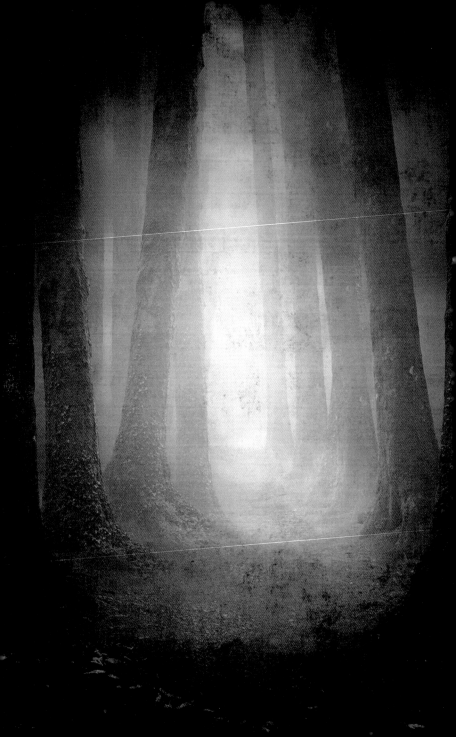

Found Grounds, Part II

The College of Charleston bought the old Bishop England Catholic High School in 1998, looking to build a better library. Surely, the land, which was once owned by the Catholic Diocese of Charleston, was clear of any issues. (Wrong.)

It wasn't completely a secret that the site where Bishop England High School was built (in 1921) was FIRST the Brown Fellowship

Society's cemetery. Yes, the high school was built on top of the cemetery. Many of the headstones in the cemetery had been moved years earlier to nearby Cunnington cemetery. The Catholic diocese—who built the high school—just assumed the bodies from the cemetery had also been moved (not just the headstones). They were wrong. (Again.) It seems the Brown Fellowship Society had a

superstition that disturbing the eternal rest of the dead could wake their spirits. So they never moved the bodies. So, stay with me here, The Catholic Diocese built a high school on top of a cemetery, and the College of Charleston was looking to knock down the high school and build a new library. On top of the cemetery.

To be fair, there are other known examples of cemeteries buried under the city. For example, there's an old Presbyterian cemetery beneath a retirement home on Market Street. The county parking garage behind the Mills House Hotel on Meeting Street is built over a seventeenth-century Quaker burial ground. So the College of Charleston wouldn't have been out of step to build on a cemetery. But what was surprising was that when they started construction, they found *four* cemeteries.

Soon after the Brown Fellowship Society's cemetery was discovered, records of eight women and one man were discovered near the site. *Their* headstones had been moved to a cemetery called Macphelah. Broken grave markers and a brick burial crypt (complete with human remains) were found on the corner of Calhoun and Coming Streets as work crews continued with construction. Turns out coroner records from 1822 to 1868 show the names of 360 people buried in Macphelah cemetery. Yes, 360!

Then TWO MORE cemeteries were found when the Macphelah cemetery was discovered. Both were old and nearly disintegrated by the time they were found.

The Catholic Diocese of Charleston paid for most of the excavation and research into the old cemeteries. They also held memorial services for the dead. A large monument was erected in front of the college's library to acknowledge the burial ground. Family members of the dead were invited to attend a special ceremony as the monument was placed.

So let's recap: bodies buried in four cemeteries were then under a high school and are now under the College of Charleston. Under your feet. Right there. Tread lightly.

Found Grounds, Part III

As we've discussed, four cemeteries were uncovered when the College of Charleston tore down the old Bishop England Catholic High School in 2000 to make way for a new, better library (ultimately the Addlestone Library). So we know there are lots of bodies underneath the College of Charleston—of the young, the old, the sick, and the unfortunate. And maybe even the presidential.

Wait, what? See, experts believe that, back in the 1960s, the college built its *previous* library on top of President Andrew Jackson's mother. Yes, you read that correctly.

Andrew Jackson tried for forty-two years to find his mother's gravesite. His mother, Elizabeth Hutchinson Jackson, had been a nurse during the American Revolution. She died in 1781, when Jackson was just a teenager, by contracting yellow fever while on duty. Jackson knew his mom was buried near the "boundary line," or city limits, of Charleston. That boundary line is now Calhoun Street.

After construction of the 1967 library was complete, historians determined that Mrs. Jackson's grave was crushed beneath it. As a giant apology—"Sorry, Mrs. Jackson!"—the college placed a monument next to the library. It reads:

Near This Spot Is Buried,
Elizabeth Jackson,
Mother of President Andrew Jackson,
She Gave Her Life Cheerfully For
The Independence of Her Country,
On An Unrecorded Date In Nov, 1781,
And To Her Son Andy This Advice:
"Andy, Never Tell A Lie,
Nor Take What Is Not Your Own,
Nor Sue For Slander,
Settle Those Cases Yourself."

So the monument is also a grave marker. One hopes that her spirit has taken the apology well.

Allison Singer is an experienced children's book editor and author from Hillsborough, NJ. She has edited books for publishers including DK and Penguin Random House, and has written a number of nonfiction titles for kids. In her current role as a Senior Editor at TIME, Allie develops content for the magazine's classroom product. Allie is currently based in Brooklyn, NY, where she spends her time reading, drinking tea, and planning adventures.

Check out some of the other Spooky America titles available now!

Spooky America was adapted from the creeptastic Haunted America series for adults. Haunted America explores historical haunts in cities and regions across America. Here's more from the original *Haunted Charleston* authors Ed Macy and Geordie Buxton:

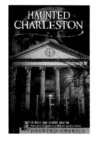